THEATRE GAMES FOR PRESCHOOL CHILDREN AGES 3-6

Creative dramatic exercises to
enhance the classroom, after school,
birthday parties, or summer camps

Theatre Games for Preschool Children Ages 3-6
Copyright ©2009 by Play-Ground Theatre Company, Inc.

FIRST EDITION
Printed in the United States of America

Published by:
Play-Ground Theatre Company, Inc.
169 Albert Drive, P.O. Box 58 Rollinsville, CO 80474
http://www.playgroundtheatre.com

THEATRE GAMES
FOR PRESCHOOL CHILDREN
AGES 3-6
FIRST EDITION

By Mia Sole & Jeff Haycock

Table of Contents

Table of Contents

Table of Contents

"Theatre is one of the primary ways children learn about life – about actions and consequences, about customs and beliefs, about others and themselves."

National Standards for Theatre Education

📖 How to use this book

This book is divided into two parts:

Part One

☺ **Circle Games**
✿ **Warm-up**
↔ **Crossing Games**
★ **Acting Games**

Each section includes fifteen theatre games that you can play with your students. Every creative dramatic exercise offers teachers easy to follow directions:

How to play
Step-by-step instructions to guide you through each game

Objective
The goal of each game

Notes
Additional information

Materials
Supplies needed for the game

Part Two

💖 **Color & Act - Emotions**

This section includes fifteen character pictures to copy and hand out. Students color the characters, then perform the five acting suggestions on the following page.

🐢 **Bonus Materials - Learning with Animals**
Try matching, spelling, and counting games with your students. Copy worksheets and make learning fun!

Play-Ground Theatre

Part One

Theatre Games for Preschool Children Ages 3-6

Circle Games, Warm-up, Crossing Games & Acting Games

Circle Games ☺

Play-Ground Theatre Circle Games

This section provides teachers with Circle Games designed to stimulate, motivate, and energize preschool children.

Play-Ground Theatre's Circle Games allow students the chance to explore their creativity, learn to communicate, develop better listening skills, and practice patience in a group setting. As you continue to play these games, you will notice improvements in students' attention spans.

Circle Games set a positive, engaging, and upbeat mood. So round up your students, and share in the joy of creative dramatics.

Circle Games Included:

Name Game

Follow the Teacher

Favorite/Least Favorite

Pass it Along

What's that Sound?

Character Circle

Positive Cheer

Zapp!

Animal Kingdom

We're Great!

Duck, Duck, Make-it-up

Emotion Circle

What are you Doing?

Share

Wiggle and Giggle

Circle Game ☺ Instructions

① Start with students sitting in a circle.

② Teacher announces the circle game.

③ Teacher gives students instructions.

④ Students have a chance to express themselves and participate with the class.

☺ Name Game

How to play

①Start with students sitting in a circle.

②Call on each student, one at a time, to say his/her name.

③After each student introduces them self, the teacher repeats the name using the suggestions below.

Note: If a student is shy, repeat the name quietly or in a whisper. If a student is outgoing, clap your hands or cheer.

④As you repeat the students' names, have the class join in.

⑤Class repeats the name three or more times.

⑥Select the next student and repeat his/her name with the class.

⑦When everyone has had a turn, the game is complete.

Name Game Suggestions

giggling	clapping	bouncing
whispering	rhythmically	wiggling
yawning	stomping	magically
sneezing	peek-a-boo-ing	stretching

Objective: Use humor and silliness to acknowledge each student.

☺ Animal Kingdom

How to play

①Start with students sitting in a circle.

②Tell students that they're going to act out different animals.

③Choose animals using the suggestions below.

④Ask the class to share what they know about each animal.

⑤Have the class make the sound of the animal.

⑥Act out three or more animals.

Note: You may ask students to share their favorite animals.

Animal Kingdom Suggestions

sheep	ferrets	elephants
cats	dogs	gorillas
lions	cows	horses
pigs	bears	donkeys
monkeys	wolves	giraffes
fox	squirrels	mice
hippos	rabbits	zebras

Objective: Learn about animals by imitating their sounds and discussing their characteristics.

☺ Follow the Teacher

How to play

①Start with students sitting in a circle.

②Tell the students that they're going to copy your movements.

③Begin by performing movements using the suggestions below.

④Students copy your movements such as flexing muscles.

⑤Have the class copy three or more movements.

Note: You may ask students to take turns leading the class or try adding vocal sounds to the movements.

Follow the Teacher Suggestions

shrugging shoulders	snapping fingers	funny sounds
touching toes	patting head	stretching arms
patting knees	yawning	pointing fingers
stretching legs	waving goodbye	nodding head
silly faces	stomping feet	clapping hands

Objective: Focus on listening skills, concentration, and following the teacher's instructions.

☺ We're Great!

How to play

①Start with students sitting in a circle.

②Ask students to place their hands in the center of the circle.

③Have the students lift up their hands and say, "Weeeeeeeeeeeeeeeeeeee're Great!"

④Ask students to place their hands in the center of the circle again.

⑤This time have the students lift up their hands and say, "Weeeeeeeeeeeeeeeeeee're smart!"

⑥Ask students to place their hands in the center again.

⑦Have the students lift up their hands and say, "Weeeeeeeeeeeeeeeeee're healthy!"

⑧Ask students to place their hands in the center again.

⑨Have the students lift up their hands and say, "Weeeeeeeeeeeeeeeeee're incredibly attractive!"

⑩Finally, ask students to place their hands in the center again, lift up their hands and say, "Weeeeeeeeeeeeeeeeeee're Great!"

Objective: Build self-esteem, confidence, team skills, and create unity in the class.

☺ Favorite/Least Favorite

How to play

①Start with students sitting in a circle.

②Tell students they're going to share their favorite and least favorite things.

③Choose a topic using the suggestions below such as foods.

④Select students, one at a time, to share their favorites.

⑤After all students have had a turn, ask them to share their least favorites.

⑥Choose three or more topics or make up your own.

Note: You may ask students to suggest additional topics.

Favorite/Least Favorite Suggestions

colors	movies	seasons
toys	games	pizza toppings
songs	activities	animals
vacations	sports	clothes

Objective: Acknowledge each student's feelings and share common interests.

☺ Duck, Duck, Make-it-up

How to play

①Start with students sitting in a circle.

②Tell students that this game is like "Duck, Duck, Goose." However, in this game each student makes up their own word for "duck" and their own word for "goose." For example: "red, red, red, PURPLE!" or "Spaghetti, spaghetti, spaghetti, MEATBALL!"

③Begin the game by walking around the circle, tapping each student on the head, saying the word of your choice.

④Say a different word when you tap the chosen student.

⑤The chosen student chases the tapper around the circle.

⑥The tapper runs around the circle to the empty seat. If the tapper is not tagged the class says, "One, two, three, SAFE!"

⑦If the tapper is tagged, everyone says, "Into the soup!" The tapper goes into the middle of the circle, and the students pretend to taste the soup.

⑧The tapper sits down and the next student takes a turn tapping around the circle.

⑨When everyone has had a turn, the game is complete.

Objective: Provide a fun, familiar game to build self-confidence, allowing students to add their own style.

☺ Pass it Along

How to play

①Start with students sitting in a circle.

②Tell students to pretend they have an invisible object in their hands.

③Instruct the class to imagine that the object can be heavy or light, soft or hard, big or small.

Note: You may want to demonstrate creating a make-believe object for students to understand the pantomime concept. For example: pretend to blow up a large balloon or struggle to pick up a heavy rock.

④After students have made their make-believe objects, have everyone toss them into the middle of the circle.

⑤The teacher reaches in and pretends to make one big object.

⑥Pretend it's heavy. Then pass it to the first student, who molds it into a new shape, and passes it to the next student in the circle.

⑦The student takes it, changes the object, passes it to the next student, and so on.

⑧When everyone has had a turn, the teacher makes the object smaller and smaller, until it disappears into the air.

> **Objective: Activate imaginations by introducing the art of pantomime.**

☺ Emotion Circle

How to play

①Start with students sitting in a circle.

②Tell students that they're going to act out different emotions.

③Select an emotion using the suggestions below such as happy.

④Demonstrate happy by smiling and giggling. Then ask students to act happy with you, smiling and giggling.

⑤Change the emotion to sad. Demonstrate sad by frowning and crying.

⑥Ask students to act sad with you, frowning and crying.

⑦Choose three or more emotions for the class to perform using the suggestions below.

Emotion Circle Suggestions

peaceful	shy	afraid	angry
tired	sick	excited	relaxed
cool	nervous	surprised	silly
sneaky	sad	crazy	happy

Objective: Learn how we process different emotions.

☺ What's that Sound?

How to play

①Start with students sitting in a circle.

②Tell students that they're going to play a game called, "What's that Sound?"

③Follow this dialog:

Teacher:　"I'll ask the questions, and you make the sounds. Okay?"

Students:　"Okay!"

Teacher:　"It's time for question number one.
　　　　　What does a _____ sound like?"

Fill in blank with suggestions below such as a train.

④Students answer the question, "Chug-a-chug-a! Chug-a-chug-a!"

⑤Teacher asks three or more questions using suggestions below.

What's that Sound? Suggestions

flock of geese	motor	helicopter
waterfall	machine	forest
jungle	radio	waves
baby	opera star	traffic

Objective: Encourage students to create sounds from their experiences.

☺ What are you Doing?

How to play

①Start with students standing in a circle.

②Begin the game by stepping in the middle of the circle, and perform an action such as watering the plants.

③The class says, "What are you doing?"

④The teacher responds, "I'm watering the plants. Everybody try!"

⑤The class performs the action (watering the plants) together.

⑥Then the teacher steps out of the circle. The first student steps in and performs a new action such as brushing hair.

⑦The class says, "What are you doing?"

⑧Student says, "I'm brushing my hair. Everybody try!"

⑨The class performs the action (brushing hair) together.

⑩The student steps out of the circle. The next student steps in and begins a new action. Repeat until everyone has had a turn.

Note: If a student has trouble performing in the circle, provide suggestions or allow them to pass.

Objective: Improve individual performance skills and develop creative thinking.

☺ Character Circle

How to play

①Start with students sitting in a circle.

②Ask students to think of their favorite character.

③Tell students that they're going to introduce themselves pretending to be their favorite characters.

④Have students raise their hands when their ready for a turn.

⑤Select a student to say their character name. and share something they like to do as that character.

⑥When each student is finished, the class says,
"Nice to meet you _____!" *Insert character name in the blank.*

⑦When everyone has had a turn, the game is complete.

Note: If a student has trouble thinking of a character they may pass, use their real name or choose from suggestions below.

Character Circle Suggestions

dragons	fairies	pirates	mermaids
kings/queens	knights	superheroes	villains
scientists	wizards	unicorns	ninjas
athletes	rock stars	dads/moms	clowns

Objective: Increase self-confidence and dramatic skills by acting as different characters.

 Share

Materials

one share per student

How to play

Note: Before playing this game, tell students to bring something from home they would like to share. For example: a book, toy, photograph, teddy bear, doll, or drawing. Teachers may also ask students to find their favorite toy in the classroom and bring it to the circle for share.

①Ask students to get their shares and sit in a circle.

②Everyone says, "Share, share, it's time for share."

③Call on students, one at a time, to share their item and talk a little bit about it.

④Ask the class to thank the student for sharing.

⑤Select the next student who is ready for a turn.

⑥When everyone has shared with the class, the game is complete.

Note: If a student doesn't have something to share, they can always tell a story or pass.

Objective: Develop verbal, interactive, and listening skills through sharing.

☺ Positive Cheer

How to play

①Start with students sitting in a circle.

②Tell students the importance of teamwork and keeping a positive attitude.

③Ask students to join you in a positive class cheer.

④Have students make a drum roll, tapping their legs to make the sound.

⑤Teacher says, "Let's hear it for _____ !"
Fill in the blank with each student's name.

⑥The student stands up, takes a bow and the class applauds.

Note: When delivering each student's name, use a nice loud stage voice and have fun with the class.

⑦When everyone has been cheered for, the game is complete.

Objective: Build self-esteem and confidence in a positive atmosphere.

☺ Wiggle and Giggle

How to play

①Start with students sitting in a circle.

②Ask students to lift up their fingers and wiggle them.

③Ask students to giggle.

④Ask students to wiggle their fingers…wiggle and giggle.

⑤Ask students to wiggle their arms… wiggle and giggle.

⑥Ask students to wiggle their legs… wiggle and giggle.

⑦Ask students to wiggle their whole body… wiggle and giggle.

⑧Tell students to raise their arms, take a deep breath in, and breathe out as they lower their arms, and let out a sigh.

Note: Use the suggestions below to wiggle other parts of the body. Students may also suggest parts of the body to wiggle.

Wiggle and Giggle Suggestions

feet	wrists	shoulders	elbows
ankles	ears	knees	noses
bottoms	hair	toes	bellies

Objective: Limber up the body and set a silly tone by wiggling and giggling.

☺ Zapp!

How to play

①Start with students sitting in a circle.

②Follow this dialog with the class:

Teacher:　"It's time to play Zapp! Everyone say Zapp!"

Students:　"Zapp!"

Teacher:　"Zapp begins with what letter?"

Students:　"Z."

Teacher:　"What else begins with the letter Z?"

Students:　"Zebra, Zipper, Zoo, Zack, Zero."

Teacher:　"Now, everyone reach up and put your hands on your head, and pull anything negative out.
For example, if you have a cold or feel tired,
pull out that bad stuff and place it in front of you."

Spend a moment pulling out bad stuff with students.

Teacher:　"Now we're going to take all this bad stuff and 'Zapp!' it into good stuff. Everyone lift up your arms, wiggle your fingers and say... Oooooooooooh Zapp!"

Students:　"Oooooooooooh Zapp!"

Teacher:　"Okay, let's try it together."

Class lifts up their arms, wiggles their fingers and says, "Zapp!"

Students: "Ooooooooooh ZAPP!"

Teacher: "One more time."

Students: "Ooooooooooh ZAPP!"

Teacher: "Last time with a little more energy!"

Students: "Ooooooooooh ZAPP!"

Teacher: "Great! Now reach down in front of you.
Scoop up all the good stuff, put it back into your head.
Sit up straight, brush your hair, fix your clothes and say,
I feel great!"

Students: "I feel great!"

Teacher: "Everyone say, I'm having a great day!"

Students: "I'm having a great day!"

Teacher: "Excellent job!"

Objective: Focus on removing negativity, replacing it with positive energy.

Warm-up

Play-Ground Theatre Warm-up

Warm-up is focused on limbering up the body, voice, and mind. Get ready to lead invigorating warm-up exercises that increase concentration and create magical environments children love.

Vocal Warm-up exercises are specially devised for students to use their imaginations, by making the sounds of animals, objects, locations, and characters.

Physical Warm-up helps the class develop coordination, rhythm, and motor skills. Jumping, stretching, and physical fitness energizes the class.

Warm-ups Included:

Stand-up, Sit-down	Fingers, Wrists and Elbows
Zing!	Jumping! Jumping! Jumping!
Reverse Zing!	The Egg
Stretch and Count	If You're Ready
Character Voices	Statue Garden
Swim Surf and Spill	Mirror Game
Nature Sounds	Building Blocks
Merry-go-round	

Warm-up ✹ Instructions

①Start with students in a circle.

②Teacher announces the Warm-up activity.

③Teacher gives students instructions.

④Students have a chance to warm-up vocally and physically.

 **Stand-up, Sit-down**

How to play

①Start with students sitting in a circle.

②Teacher says, "Okay everybody it's time to warm-up. So, let's all stand up!" Teacher and students stand up.

③Teacher says, "Great job everyone! Wait a minute, I think we're supposed to sit down." Teacher and students sit down.

④Teacher says, "Hold on a second (teacher pauses and thinks), we start standing up." All students stands up.

⑤Teacher says, "No, it was sitting." All students sit down again.

⑥Teacher continues to change his/her mind while the class stands up and sits down, over and over again.

⑦To end the game students say, "This is getting ridiculous!"

Objective: Create a joyous, comfortable atmosphere that's fun and silly.

 Fingers, Wrists and Elbows

How to play

①Start with students standing up.

②Tell students to lift up their hands, wiggle their fingers and say, "fingers."

③Tell students to circle their wrists and say, "wrists."

④Tell students to bend both elbows up and down and say, "elbows, elbows, elbows, elbows."

⑤Tell students to shrug their shoulders and say, "I don't know."

⑥Ask students to shrug their shoulders and say, "I don't know" three or more times, building intensity.

⑦Have students raise their hands, jump up and down and say, "Wait, I know!"

⑧Tell students to stretch up to the sky, take a big breath and exhale.

Note: You may add different motions. For example: bending the knees, shaking out the legs, rolling the neck, or circling the ankles.

Objective: Warm-up the voice and body with simple movements.

 # Zing!

How to play

①Start with students standing up.

②Tell students to lift their arms and magically wiggle their fingers.

③Explain that they will shoot magic from their fingertips towards the teacher and say, "Zing!"

④Teacher counts to three and the students "Zing!" their magical energy.

⑤The teacher reacts by jumping back, acting surprised at the magical powers of the class.

Note: For this exercise the most important thing is to play up the magical power of the class. With each "Zing!" react as if the classes power is pushing you back further and further.

⑥Ask the class "Zing!" you three or more times, building their intensity.

⑦Compliment students on their magical abilities.

Objective: Empower the class, acknowledging their energy and magical abilities.

☀ Jumping! Jumping! Jumping!

How to play

①Start with students standing up.

②Tell students that they're going to jump up and down together, then "FREEZE!"

③Ask students to jump up down while saying, "Jumping! Jumping! Jumping! Jumping! Jumping! Jumping! FREEZE!"

④Repeat this three or more times, encouraging students to get better at freezing.

⑤The last time the students jump up and down, ask to them to "FREEZE!" the best they can.

⑥Compliment the class on their jumping and freezing skills.

Note: When the class is familiar with this warm-up, try different variations using suggestions below.

Jumping! Jumping! Jumping! Suggestions

on one foot   jumping beans

baby bunnies   bouncing balls

kangaroos   grasshoppers

frogs   on pogo sticks

Objective: Warm-up and activate responsiveness.

 Reverse Zing!

How to play

①Start with students standing up.

②Tell students to lift their arms and magically wiggle their fingers.

③Explain that they will shoot magic from their fingertips towards the teacher and say, "Zing!"

④The teacher counts to three and the students "Zing!" their magical energy.

⑤The teacher reacts by jumping back, acting surprised at the magical powers of the class.

⑥Teacher reverses the "Zing!" and students jump backwards, reacting to the teacher's magical power.

⑦Repeat this three or more times.

Note: For this exercise the most important thing is to play up your power. Each time you "Zing!" the students, they jump back further, reacting to your increased magical abilities.

Objective: Acknowledge the teacher's energy and magical abilities.

 # The Egg

How to play

①Ask students to find a place on the floor and to get into an egg position by crouching down, tucking their heads in.

②Tell students to say, "Don't talk to me, I'm in my egg." Then say, "I'm very busy in my egg." Finally say, "Just call my cell phone, I'm in my egg." Then have students return to the egg position.

③Choose an action to perform using the suggestions below.

④Ask the class to count to three, then rise up from their egg positions and perform together. Allow the class to act for a few moments.

⑤Tell the class to say, "Back to the egg!" Then students return to the egg position.

⑥Choose three or more actions using the suggestions below.

Note: You may play a favorite piece of instrumental music to enhance this game.

Egg Suggestions

Grow like seeds, slowly stretching up to the sky and blooming.
Turn into robots walking and talking.
Swim like fish in the ocean.
Grow into giants and stomp around.
Fly like hummingbirds.
Take a puppy for a walk.

Objective: Develop the ability to form images in the mind, then perform them.

 Stretch and Count

How to play

①Start with students sitting in a circle.

②Ask students to take a big breath in, lift up their arms and stretch while counting to three.

③Ask student to breath in again, bend over and touch their toes while counting to five.

④Ask students to stand up, lift their arms to the sky while counting to seven.

⑤Ask students to stretch their arms to the sides and make little arm circles while counting to ten.

⑥Ask students to sit down, stretch out their legs and slowly bend over to touch their toes while counting to four.

⑦Finally, ask students to stand up, stretch their arms to the sky while counting backwards from ten. Then lower their arms and say, "Aaaaaaaahhhhhhh."

Note: You can vary the stretches or the numbers the class counts to. You may also ask students to suggest a stretch or a number to count to.

Objective: Stretching muscles while increasing counting skills.

 If You're Ready

How to play

● Start with students standing up.

● Tell students to listen to instructions and follow your movements.

● Teacher repeats the following lines with a loud voice, rhythmically while performing the motions.

"If you're ready put your hands on your head!
Teacher and students put hands on head.

If you're ready put your hands on your nose!
Teacher and students put hands on nose.

If you're ready put your hands on your knees!
Teacher and students put hands on knees.

If you're ready put your hands on your toes. Knees! Toes!
Teacher and students put hands on toes, then knees and toes.

Knees! Toes! If you're ready say… I'm READY!"
Teacher and students put hands on knees and toes.

● Students mirror the actions and say, "I'm READY!"

Note: This warm-up is a great way to focus students at any time, or as a transition from one activity to another. You may also want to vary the commands. For example: "If you're ready put your hands on your hips, elbows, shoulders, hair, or ankles."

Objective: Focus the student's attention, uniting the class with an upbeat, positive attitude.

 # Character Voices

How to play

①Start with students standing up.

②Tell students they're going to repeat lines using character voices.

③Select three or more lines to repeat with the class using the suggestions below.

④Ask students to raise their hands if they want to make up a character line for the class to repeat.

Note: Feel free to create new character voices or lines.

⑤When everyone has had a turn to lead, the game is complete.

Character	Line
Knight	"Hark! Who goes there!"
Cowboy/girl	"Howdy partners! Let's ride, rope and wrangle."
Pirate	"Ahoy thar maties. How in the salty sea ye be?"
Caveman	"Unga bunga! Unga bunga bunga!"
Baby	"Goo goo ga ga goo goo. I want my bottle!"
Superhero	"Don't worry. I'll save you!"
Leprechaun	"Have you seen my pot of gold?

Objective: Encourage vocal expression and develop character-acting skills.

 # Statue Garden

How to play

①Start with students standing up together as if they're on stage.

②Tell students that they're going to pretend to be statues in a statue garden.

③Announce the title of the Statue Garden using the suggestions below. Then ask students to turn around.

④On the count of three, the class turns back around, facing the audience while striking a statue pose.

⑤Clap for students and announce another Statue Garden title.

⑥Give the class three or more titles to perform using the suggestions below or make up your own.

Statue Garden Suggestions

deep in the ocean	wizard's wand	surprise party
farm animals	silly clowns	rock stars
a garden full of flowers	stinky socks	at a tea party
big dinosaurs	teddy bear picnic	the rollercoaster
lost in the woods	puppy power	funny faces

Objective: Coach the class in quick, creative thinking while using pantomime.

 Swim, Surf and Spill

How to play

①Ask the students to stand in a circle.

②Tell students that they're going to use their imaginations and pretend to go on a trip the beach.

③Ask students to pretend to put on their swimsuits. Then slowly dip their toes in the water and say, "Oh, the water is chilly!"

④Ask students to grab their make-believe surfboards, dive in to the ocean and swim in place using their arms.

⑤Have students say, "Here comes a big wave, let's surf it!"

⑥Ask students to jump on their surfboards and ride the wave.

⑦Have students spill off their surfboards and say, "Total wipe out!"

⑧Ask students to repeat surfing and spilling a few more times.

⑨To end the warm-up, have the class say, "Wow! What a ride!"

Note: You may try adding different scenarios while swimming. For example: swimming with dolphins, spotting a group of mermaids, water skiing, or dodging sharks in the water.

Objective: Use the imagination to warm-up the body.

 # Mirror Game

How to play

①Start with students standing up.

②Ask students to copy your movements as if they're looking in a mirror.

③Demonstrate an action slowly, like stretching your arms above your head, then lowering them down to your sides.

④Ask students to follow and mirror the action.

⑤Lead the class with three or more actions using the suggestions below. Then select students who would like a turn to lead the group.

⑥The class mirrors each student.

⑦When everyone has had a turn, the game is complete.

Mirror Game Suggestions

running in place	in slow motion	dancing
jumping jacks	blowing up a balloon	picking apples
waving hello	sleep walking	doing ballet
on a balance beam	eating a banana	on one foot
marching	playing an instrument	making a cake

Objective: Improve concentration and promote working together.

 Nature Sounds

How to play

①Start with students sitting in a circle.

②Tell students that they're going to make different nature sounds.

③Select a sound using the suggestions below and allow a few moments to create the environment vocally.

④Ask students to listen for instructions as you guide them through the sound qualities listed below.

⑤Choose three or more sounds to perform.

Nature Sounds Suggestions	Sound Qualities
wind blowing	soft, medium, strong
baby birds calling for food	quietly and loudly
rain falling	gently, hard with thunder
waves on the ocean	small ones, big ones, tidal
wolves howling at the moon	soft, medium, loud
lions	soft purr, loud roar
bees, buzzing	soft, medium, loud

Objective: Explore nature through creating environments and vocalizations.

 # Building Blocks

How to play

①Start with students standing up.

②Tell students that they're going to build things together.

③Ask students to collect make-believe materials and have them pretend to build a house together.

④When the house is complete, ask the class to say, "Let's build something else."

⑤Ask students to gather materials to build a swimming pool.

⑥Have students build a swimming pool together and fill it up with make-believe water. When the swimming pool is complete, ask the class to take a dip.

⑦Have students say, "A job well done!"

Note: Use suggestions below for additional things to build.

Building Block Suggestions

candy store	campfire	sand castle	barn
space ship	tree house	circus tent	carousel
sky scraper	ocean liner	veggie garden	bridge

Objective: Support creative cooperation and teamwork.

 Merry-go-round

How to play

①Start with students standing in a circle.

②Tell students that they're going to act together while revolving in a circle, like a merry-go-round.

③Ask students to hold hands and circle around to the right.

④Ask students to stop and circle around to the left.

⑤Ask students to stop and let go of each other's hands.

⑥Tell the class to say, "All aboard!" and become a train. Then chug-a-chug-a around to the right, hit the brakes and around to the left.

⑦Tell students to say, "Giddy-up!" and get on their make-believe horses. Then ride around to the right, pull the reins and say, "Whoa!" and ride around to the left.

⑧Ask students to dance around to the right, and dance around to the left. End the game with students clapping for each other.

Note: You may ask students for additional suggestions or add your own ideas.

Objective: Promote joy-filled teamwork by acting and dancing in the round.

Changing the world
one child at a time

Play-Ground
Theatre

Crossing
Games

Play-Ground Theatre Crossing Games

Play-Ground Theatre Crossing Games connect students by allowing everyone to pretend and participate together. They offer students a chance to cross the space, exploring different emotions, people, animals, or characters. This fuses physical and artistic expression with creative movement.

Students are instructed to raise their hands if they would like a turn. The student receives instructions and leads the group or suggests an idea and crosses the space while the class follows. When the class has crossed the space, the teacher selects another student.
If a student would not like a turn, they may pass.

Crossing Games Included:

How Things Move	Copy Cat
Emotion Crossing	Walking Through
Character Crossing	Four Seasons
Animal Crossing	Sports Stars
Greeting Game	Going on a Trip
Action/Reaction	Costume Closet
Locations	Stages of Life
Working out the Bugs	

Crossing Game ⟷ Instructions

Wall #1

Students cross
from wall #1 to wall #2

Wall #2

①Start with students lined up, ready to act.

②Teacher gives instructions for Crossing Game.

③Students take turns leading the group.

④Students cross the space acting.

⑤Then students line up for the next turn.

←→How Things Move

How to play

①Start with students lined up, ready to act.

②Ask the students to think of a way to cross the space.

③Select a student to share his/her idea such as jumping.

④Have the class cross the space performing the student's suggestion, for this example jumping.

⑤Ask students to line up and raise their hands if they know another way to cross.

⑥The next student has a turn to give a new suggestion.

⑦When everyone has had a turn to lead the class, the game is complete.

Note: If students need assistance, use the suggestions below.

How Things Move Suggestions

spinning	slithering	jogging	flying
sneaking	tip-toeing	backwards	crab walking
leaping	baby stepping	crawling	skipping
jumping	rolling	giant steps	floating

Objective: Explore creative movement.

Copy Cat

How to play

①Start with students lined up, ready to act.

②Tell students that they're going to copy the actions of the person who is leading.

③Begin the game by asking students to copy your movements, and skip across the space as the class follows you.

④Ask students to raise their hands when they're ready for a turn to lead.

Note: Tell students that they can speak or make sounds along with their movements.

⑤Select a student to lead the class across the space. Remind everyone to copy the leader's movements as closely as possible.

⑥When everyone has had a turn to lead the class, the game is complete.

Note: Ask the class to quiet down and pay attention between turns. Encourage everyone to be polite to each other and they will be rewarded with a chance to lead the class.

Objective: Promote individuality, leadership and politeness.

←→Emotion Crossing

How to play

①Start with students lined up, ready to act.

②Tell students that they're going to cross the space performing an emotion. Explain that an emotion is the way you feel about something such as happy, sad, shy, or angry.

③Select a student to share an emotion for the class to perform or use the suggestions below.

④Ask the class to cross the room acting out the student's suggestion.

Note: If students need more guidance, discuss each emotion before the students cross the space or demonstrate for the class.

⑤After the class crosses the space, choose another student.

⑥When everyone has had a turn, the game is complete.

Emotion Crossing Suggestions

sick	happy	angry	stubborn
sad	nervous	excited	hot
surprised	afraid	silly	serious
curious	shy	cool	peaceful

Objective: Explore different emotions through dramatic play.

←→Walking Through

How to play

①Start with students lined up, ready to act.

②Tell students that they're going to walk through different things.

③Start the game by asking students to cross the space pretending to be walking through a snowstorm.

④After students cross, ask them to line up and listen for instructions.

⑤Choose three or more things to walk through using the suggestions below.

Note: You may ask students to suggest other things to cross through.

Walking Through Suggestions

banana peels	jumpy castle	the center of the earth
desert	spider web	puffy clouds
hot lava	bubble gum	magical forest
sprinkler	spaghetti	busy city
rainbow	mud	tall grass
super glue	feathers	marbles

Objective: Create imaginary environments through different movements.

←→Character Crossing

How to play

①Start with students lined up, ready to act.

②Tell students that they're going to cross the space performing different characters.

③Choose a character for students to perform using the suggestions below such as little elves.

④Between each turn, ask students to line up, listening for the next instruction.

⑤Have students cross as three or more characters.

Note: You may ask students to share character suggestions or make up your own.

Character Crossing Suggestions

superheroes	rodeo cowboys	magic genies
basketball players	Olympic athletes	circus clowns
airplane pilots	magical fairies	brave knights
flying ghosts	secret agents	cool rappers
tap dancers	old farmers	court jesters

Objective: Enhance character development through movement.

←→Four Seasons

How to play

①Start with students lined up, ready to act.

②Ask students to think of an activity they like to do in the winter.

③Call on a student to share an activity for the class to perform.

④Have students cross the space performing the student's suggestion such as ice-skating.

⑤Ask the class to line up and select a new student to share another activity.

⑥Students cross the space performing as many winter activities as they can suggest.

⑦When everyone has had a turn, change the question to:

- What activities do you like to do in the spring?

- What activities do you like to do in the summer?

- What activities do you like to do in the fall?

⑧When students have performed activities from all four seasons, the game is complete.

Objective: Learn about the seasons through discussion and creative movement.

←→Animal Crossing

How to play

①Start with students lined up, ready to act.

②Tell students to think of an animal they would like to perform.

③Choose students, one at a time, to suggest an animal or use the suggestions below.

④Ask students to cross the space acting like that animal such as a hippopotamus.

Note: If students need guidance, spend time discussing the characteristics of each animal before crossing the space.

⑤When the class has crossed the space, select a new student to suggest another animal.

⑥When everyone has selected an animal, the game is complete.

Animal Crossing Suggestions

kittens	wolves	beavers	goats
skunks	rabbits	panda bears	tigers
raccoons	porcupines	squirrels	zebras
hamsters	deer	gorillas	kangaroos

Objective: Learn about animals through movements and vocalizations.

←→Sports Stars

How to play

①Start with students lined up, ready to act.

②Ask students to think of their favorite sport.

③Students raise their hands when they are ready for a turn.

④Select a student to announce his/her sport or use the suggestions below.

⑤Students cross the space pretending to play that sport.

⑥At the end of each turn, ask one or two students to demonstrate the sport in front of the class.

⑦Select another student to suggest a different sport and cross playing.

⑧When everyone has had a turn, the game is complete.

Sports Stars Suggestions

football	hockey	baseball	kickball
lacrosse	tennis	bowling	basketball
volleyball	skiing	weight lifting	field hockey
gymnastics	water skiing	horse racing	golfing

Objective: Assimilate athletic skills with creative dramatic play.

←→Greeting Game

How to play

①Start by asking students to find a partner.

②Ask students to form two lines on opposite sides of the space, with partners facing each other. Tell students that partners will greet each other in the center of the space, and cross to the opposite line.

③Ask for a volunteer and demonstrate greeting each other in a friendly manner, then cross to the opposite side of the space (see the Greeting Game Formation below).

④Instruct students to cross the space, greet their partner in a friendly manner, and then go to the opposite line.

⑤Announce three or more greetings for pairs to perform using the suggestions on the following page, or mix and match them.

⑥At the end of each turn, ask one pair of students to demonstrate the greeting for the class.

Note: You may ask students to suggest additional greetings for the class to perform.

Greeting Game Formation

Greeting Game Suggestions

sleepy	in slow motion	in a hurry
on a magic carpet	very hungry	with the hiccups
politely	sadly	surprised
cold	mountain climbers	excited
aliens	little fish	ballerinas
scientists	secret agents	dancing
karate masters	horseback riders	clowns
happy	laughing	shy
silly	soldiers	klutzes
surfing	ghosts	giants
with a limp	walking a dog	looking for something
roller-skating	ninjas	babies
teddy bears	race cars	robots
skipping	picking flowers	flying
floating on a cloud	on motorcycles	hopping
jumping rope	jogging	playing an instrument

Objective: Improve social skills by interacting with a partner in a variety of ways.

←→Going on a Trip

How to play

①Start with students lined up, ready to act.

②Ask students to raise their hands if they have ever taken a trip.

③Tell students that they're going to cross the space pretending to go on a trip.

④Ask students to raise their hands to suggest a place they would like the class to go. Select a student to choose a destination.

⑤Then ask students the following questions:

- What would we see on this trip?

- How would we get to this place?

- What would we do there?

⑥After the questions are answered, the class crosses the space pretending to visit that destination.

⑦Select another student and choose a place to go.

⑧When everyone has had a turn to suggest a travel destination, the game is complete.

Objective: Learn about traveling by going to make-believe destinations.

←→Action/Reaction

How to play

①Start with students lined up, ready to act.

②Tell students to cross the space like they're cute little bees.

③Ask students to line up, listening for the next instruction.

④Tell students to cross again as if bees are chasing them.

⑤After students line up, select three or more scenarios using the suggestions below.

Note: You may ask students to create other Action/Reaction suggestions.

Action/Reaction Suggestions

as giants/hiding from giants

as rabbits eating in a garden/as farmers chasing rabbits out of garden

swimming like sharks/swimming away from sharks

as dinosaurs stomping/as cave people running away from dinosaurs

putting out a fire/running from a fire

climbing up a mountain/falling down a mountain

Objective: Introduce students to acting and reacting to dramatic situations.

←→Costume Closet

How to play

①Start with students lined up, ready to act.

②Tell students that it's time play the Costume Closet game, where you can wear any costume imaginable.

③Ask students to reach up and open the closet door.

④Have the students reach in and pull out an animal costume, then pretend to put it on.

⑤Ask students to cross as animals and then return to the closet.

⑥Have students take off their animal costumes and hang them back up.

⑦Then ask students to pull out a magical costume.

⑧Have students magically fly across the space, return to the closet, and hang up costumes again.

⑨Choose as many costumes as you wish, before closing the closet door and saying, "See you next time."

Objective: Foster the imagination through make-believe dress up time.

Locations

How to play

①Start with students lined up, ready to act.

②Tell students that they're going to cross the space pretending they're in different locations.

③Select the first location using the suggestions below.

④Have students cross the space acting as if they're in that location.

⑤Ask students to line up, listening for the next instruction.

⑥Have students act out three or more locations using the suggestions below.

Note: You may ask students to suggest locations or make up your own.

Location Suggestions

swimming pool	dark cave	on the moon
candy store	frozen pond	horse ranch
football game	ocean	amusement park
mountain top	haunted house	toy shop

Objective: Travel to different locations and share your experiences.

←→Stages of Life

How to play

①Start with students lined up, ready to act.

②Tell students that they're going to perform the stages of life.

③Ask students about each stage of life using the dialog below.

④Ask a question and select a student to answer.

⑤Cross the space acting out each stage of life, and then ask students the next question.

⑥When all stages of life have been performed, the game is complete.

Stages of Life Dialog

Teacher: "What is the first thing that happens to you in life?"
Students: "You are born."
Teacher: "Right, let's cross the room as if we were just born."
Class crosses the space with teacher.

Teacher: "Then you begin to crawl, and you are called?"
Students: "Babies."
Teacher: "That's right, let's all cross the room as babies."
Class crosses the space with teacher – crawling.

Note: Remember to ask the class about each stage of life.
For example: What do babies do? or What do adults do?
This provides the class with ideas on how to cross the space.

Teacher: "After you're babies, you get bigger and you are…?"
Students: "Toddlers."
Teacher: "Yes, let's all cross like we're toddlers."
Class crosses the space with teacher – toddling.

Teacher: "Then after that, you get a little bigger, you are called?"
Students: "Kids."
Teacher: "That's right, let's all cross like we're kids."
Class crosses the space with teacher – playing.

Teacher: "After your kids, what is the next stage of life?"
Students: "Teenagers."
Teacher: "Yes, let's all cross like teenagers."
Class crosses the space with teacher – as teenagers.

Teacher: "Then you grow up even more, and you become?"
Students: "Adults."
Teacher: "That's right, let's all cross like adults."
Class crosses the space with teacher – as adults.

Teacher: "What is the next stage of life, after adults?"
Students: "Grandparents."
Teacher: "Yes, let's all cross like grandparents."
Class crosses the space with teacher – as grandparents.

Teacher: "We were born, we were babies, toddlers, kids,
             teenagers, adults, grandparents, and then what
             happens after that?"
Students: "You die."
Teacher: "That's right, let's all cross the space pretending to die."
Class crosses the space with teacher – dying.

Teacher: "Then what happens?"
Students: "You fly like angels."
Teachers: "Yes! Everyone fly around like angels."
Class crosses the space with teacher – flying.

***Objectives: Increase knowledge of life's stages through acting
and discussion.***

←→Working out the Bugs

How to play

①Start with students lined up, ready to act.

②Ask the students to think of a bug they're familiar with.

③Select a student to share a bug for the class to perform.

④Have the class share what they know about the bug, and then cross the space performing the student's suggestion such as crickets.

⑤Ask the class to line up and a new student is selected for a turn.

⑥Students cross the space performing as many bugs as they can suggest.

⑦When everyone has had a turn, the game is complete.

Note: If a student needs help thinking of bugs, you may use the suggestions below.

Working out the Bugs Suggestions

ants	ladybugs	beetles	fireflies
caterpillars	spiders	stink bugs	butterflies
cockroaches	house flies	mosquitoes	moths
centipedes	praying mantis	dragonflies	grasshoppers

Objective: Learn about bugs through discussion and creative movement.

Changing the world
one child at a time ®

Play-Ground
Theatre

Acting Games ★	# Play-Ground Theatre Acting Games

Play-Ground Theatre Acting Games offer students an opportunity to share their creative expression and sharpen their dramatic abilities, in a supportive atmosphere. They teach students stage presence, line delivery, characterization, and cultivate self-confidence. During the Acting Games, students who are not on stage represent the audience. This helps students learn to be polite as well as teaches the students on stage how to entertain their peers.

To keep the students involved and courteous to the actors, you will use an animated and effective technique called, "AND ACTION!" Each time students perform, the audience is instructed to begin the scene with the phrase, "AND ACTION!" Demonstrate this by swinging the arm forward and pointing the index finger to the stage area.

Acting Games Included:

All Together Now	Who are you? What do you do?
Sneaky Duck Down	Actor and Audience
Magic Hat	Age Game
Entrance Game	Animals and Emotions
Solo Scenes	Prop Game
Phone Game	Pictures
Newspaper Game	Jumping Bean Story
Jumping Bean Treasure	

Acting Game Instructions

X X X X X X X X X X X X

X = Students sit together to form the audience

Stage area where students
perform the Acting Games

①Start with students sitting to form the audience.

②Teacher gives instructions and goes over the stage
rules:
- Always face the audience.
- Speak clearly and in a nice, loud voice.
- Have fun on stage!

③Remind students in the audience to be polite and
quiet.

④Begin each turn with the line, "AND ACTION!"

⑤Students take turns performing for each other.

 # ★ All Together Now

How to play

①Start with students sitting down for instructions.

②Tell students that they're going to act out different things together.

③Ask students to perform an action together using the suggestions below such as a box of kittens.

④When everyone is ready to begin, students are instructed to say, "AND ACTION!"

⑤The class performs the scene for a few moments until the "FREEZE!" cue is given, and a new action is selected.

⑥Perform three or more actions using the suggestions below.

Note: If you have two teachers, you may try this activity as a guessing game. Teacher one leaves the room. The second teacher selects and performs the suggestion with the class. Teacher one returns and guesses the action.

All Together Now Suggestions

fish in a tank	baby chicks hatching	pine forest
popcorn popping	washing machine	bees in a hive
toys on a shelf	flock of geese	a thunder cloud
a long fence	ocean waves	trick or treating

Objective: Perform a short scene with the entire class.

# ★ Who are you? What do you do?

How to play

①Start with students sitting down to form the audience.

②Ask students to choose a character that they would like to perform.

③Teacher demonstrates acting as a character on stage and interacts with the audience.

Note: For example, if you were demonstrating a Queen, enter the stage in character, facing the audience. Then introduce yourself with a strong voice, tell what you do as a Queen, bow and exit.

④Select a student to enter the stage as the class claps and says, "Who are you? What do you do?"

⑤The teacher and student on stage exchange this dialog:

Teacher:　　"Who are you?"
Student:　　"I'm a puppy named Spot."
Teacher:　　"What do you do?"
Student:　　"I like to eat bones and do tricks."
Teacher:　　"Would you like to do some tricks?"
Student:　　"Okay." (Student does tricks.)
Class:　　　"It's nice to meet you!" (Student bows and sits.)

⑥Select another student and begin again.

⑦When everyone has had a turn, the game is complete.

> ***Objective: Learn interaction with an audience and portray a character on stage.***

★ Sneaky Duck Down

How to play

①Start with students sitting down for instructions. Tell the class that they're going to perform a sneaky story.

②Tell students that the teacher pretends to be lost in the forest as the class sneaks slowly behind.

③The teacher pretends to be afraid. Suddenly he/she hears something, turns around and says, "What was that?!"

④The class quickly DUCKS DOWN and FREEZES. The teacher pretends not to see the students and says, "Must have been my imagination."

⑤The teacher continues on as the students sneak behind. The teacher stops again and says, "What was that!"

⑥The class DUCKS DOWN and FREEZES again. The teacher still doesn't see anything and says, "I'm getting a little scared."

⑦Students continue to act this out, sneaking and ducking down.

⑧Finally, instruct the students to jump up and say, "SURPRISE!" after the teacher says, "WHAT WAS THAT!"

Note: Play up the dramatic tension when the students duck down. The class may wish to add sounds as they sneak. For example: the wind, giggling, howling, or roaring.

Objective: Synchronize timing, movement, and dramatic tension to create suspense and comedy.

 Actor and Audience

How to play

①Start by dividing the class in half. Ask half the class to sit down to form the audience, and the other half to stand up on the stage to become the actors.

②Ask the actors to enter the stage, face the audience and say, "Hello audience!" Tell the audience to respond by saying, "Hello actors!"

③Select an action for the actors to perform using the suggestions below. Start by having the class say, "AND ACTION!"

④After a few moments, instruct the actors to "FREEZE!" and select a different action to perform. Start again by saying, "AND ACTION!"

⑤Actors on stage perform three or more actions, then bow as the audience applauds.

⑥Switch the groups, so the students in the audience become the actors on stage, and begin again.

Actor and Audience Suggestions

taking pictures	playing baseball	sleep walking
butterflies	brushing teeth	cooking lunch
learning to swim	watering a garden	opening a gift
paddling canoes	flying kites	eating ice cream
writing letters	sawing wood	lifting weights
making funny faces	sleeping in a tent	painting

> *Objective: Introduce audience participation and fundamental acting skills.*

 Magic Hat

Materials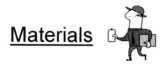

a hat
Magic Hat Suggestions (see next page)

How to play

①Copy, cut, and place Magic Hat Suggestions inside the hat or make up your own.

②Ask students to sit down and listen to instructions.

③Tell students they will have a chance to pick an action from the Magic Hat.

④Ask students to give their magic to the hat by wiggling their fingers and saying, "Zing!" Teacher reacts to the student's magic.

⑤Students take turns picking actions out of the hat.

⑥Teacher reads the action and performs it with the class.

⑦When everyone has picked from the hat, the game is complete.

Note: You may play this as a guessing game. Have the students perform and the audience guesses what the action is.

Objective: Develop acting skills and share talents with others.

Magic Hat Suggestions – Copy, cut, and place in hat.

playing baseball	building a sand castle
catching a fish	picking flowers
painting a picture	singing a song
reading a book	sky diving
milking a cow	swimming
sleep walking	riding a bike
dancing a jig	driving a race car
eating a lollypop	playing a video game
playing basketball	cooking
landing a spaceship	grooming a dog

 Age Game

How to play

①Start with students finding a partner and sitting for instructions.

②Tell students that each pair must choose the same age, between one and one hundred years, to perform. This age must be kept secret.

③Pairs that are ready raise their hands. Ask each pair of actors to whisper their age to you, before the scene begins.

④Begin each turn by saying, "AND ACTION!" Allow each pair to act for a few moments then say, "FREEZE!"

⑤Ask students in the audience to raise their hands to guess the age being performed. If the correct age is higher than the age guessed, tell the class, "higher." If the correct age is lower than the age guessed, tell the class, "lower."

⑥When the correct age is guessed, actors bow, the audience applauds and the next pair has a turn.

Note: Each pair performs a short scene, so remind the audience to remain quiet and polite until the "FREEZE!" cue is given.

⑦After each pair has had a turn, students may want to choose a new age to perform.

Objective: Gain an understanding of different ages through performance.

 **Entrance Game**

How to play

①Start with students finding a partner and sitting for instructions.

②Each pair is given an entrance to perform using the suggestions below. This must be kept secret from the audience.

③Students raise their hands when they are ready for a turn.

④Choose the first pair of students and quietly instruct them on how to enter the stage. Make sure the class does not hear.

⑤Students in the audience give actors the cue, "AND ACTION!" to begin each turn.

⑥The actors enter as instructed, after a few moments, the "FREEZE!" cue is given, and the audience guesses the action.

⑦When the correct answer is given, ask students on stage to bow, audience applauds, and the next pair has a turn. After each pair has had a turn, the game is complete.

Entrance Game Suggestions

playing tag	climbing a mountain	walking backwards
sailing a boat	digging a hole	hitting a home run
inchworms	astronauts	swinging on swings
train engineers	telling secrets	making a snowman
playing guitars	scuba divers	tight rope walkers
flying a kite	cutting grass	baby sitters

Objective: Communicate an action or character while entering the stage with a partner.

 **Animals and Emotions**

How to play

①Start with students finding a partner and sitting for instructions.

②Each pair is given an animal and an emotion to perform using the suggestions below. This must be kept secret from the audience.

③The audience says, "AND ACTION!" to begin each turn.

④Pairs act out both the animal and the emotion together such as excited fish, stubborn roosters, or nervous skunks.

⑤Ask the class to guess what the students are performing.

⑥When the correct answer is given, choose a new pair to perform.

⑦When each pair has had a turn, the game is complete.

Note: Try this game with characters and emotions such as angry ballerinas.

Animal Suggestions

bears	monkeys	cheetahs
whales	tigers	cows
kittens	eagles	horses
deer	skunks	ducks
goats	roosters	camels

Emotion Suggestions

happy	hot	shy
silly	afraid	sad
excited	angry	cold
nervous	stubborn	sick
surprised	crazy	tired

Objective: Combine animals and emotions to create silly scenes and portray hilarious characters.

 **Solo Scenes**

How to play

①Start with students sitting to form the audience.

②Select a student to perform an action on stage using the suggestions below.

③The audience begins the scene by saying, "AND ACTION!"

④The student performs the action for a few moments, then takes a bow as the audience applauds.

⑤Select a new student to take the stage and choose a different suggestion for him/her to perform.

⑥When everyone has had a turn, the game is complete.

Solo Scene Suggestions

sweeping the floor	making a bed	taking a bath
cleaning your room	digging in a garden	brushing your teeth
raking leaves	feeding a pet	doing exercises
making cup cakes	picking flowers	on a trampoline
shoveling snow	riding a horse	eating cereal

Objective: Increase confidence and stage presence.

★ Prop Game

Materials

props - for example: toys, costumes, stuffed animals, puppets, microphone, wigs, hats, etc.

How to play

①Collect one prop for each student playing the game.

②Start with students sitting down for instructions.

③Tell students that they're going to perform a scene with a prop.

④Place a prop on stage and select a student to perform with it.

⑤The audience begins each turn by saying, "AND ACTION!"

⑥Student performs with the prop for a few moments, then bows as the audience applauds.

⑦Select a new student to take the stage, and choose a different prop for him/her to perform with.

⑧When everyone has had a turn, the game is complete.

Note: Try this with partners, when the object of the game is to share the prop in a short scene.

> ***Objective: Introduce props to stimulate imagination and improvisation skills.***

★ Phone Game

Materials

toy or old telephone

How to play

①Start with students sitting down for instructions. Tell students that they're going to take turns pretending to talk on the phone.

②Ask students to raise their hands when they're ready for a turn.

③Select a student and tell him/her who is calling using the suggestions below.

④Ask the audience to ring the phone three times, before the student answers.

⑤The student says, "Hello?" then pretends to have a short conversation. At the end of the call, the student says, "Thanks for calling. Bye." Finally, the student hangs up the phone.

⑥When everyone has had a turn, the game is complete.

Phone Game Suggestions

mom is calling	dad is calling	teacher is calling
grandma is calling	big bird is calling	grandpa is calling
movie star is calling	tooth fairy is calling	babysitter is calling
Santa is calling	doctor is calling	President is calling

Objective: Learn phone conversation and communication skills.

★ Pictures

Materials

paper - one sheet per student
crayons or markers

How to play

①Start with students sitting down for instructions.

②Ask students to think of a favorite character.

③Tell students that they're going to draw a picture of that character.

④Ask students to write their names on the back of their paper, and remind everyone to share the crayons or markers provided.

⑤Ask students to draw pictures.

⑥Collect pictures and ask students to sit down, forming the audience.

⑦Call students up, one at a time, to show their picture, act out their character, or tell a little bit about it.

Note: Remember to compliment each student's artwork.

⑧When everyone has had a turn, the game is complete.

Objective: Nurture and cultivate self-expression through drawing.

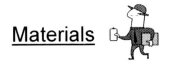 Newspaper Game

Materials

newspaper - one sheet per student

How to play

①Start with students sitting down for instructions.

②Tell students that they're going to make a prop or make-believe object with a piece of newspaper.

③Before distributing the newspapers, demonstrate the game by rolling up a piece, and using it as a telescope.

④Then give each student newspaper and a few moments to create their own special prop. Tell students they may fold, tear, crumple, or manipulate paper in any way they wish.

Note: You may want to demonstrate additional newspaper props. For example: a hat, boat, airplane, or flower.

⑤Select a student to show their newspaper creation.

⑥Student introduces his/her prop and performs with it.

⑦When everyone has had a turn, the game is complete.

Objective: Strengthen the imagination by creating a prop with a sheet of newspaper.

★ Jumping Bean Story

How to play

①Start with students sitting down for instructions.

②Tell students that they're going to perform the "Jumping Bean Story."

③Teacher reads the story and the students portray the jumping beans, repeating those lines.

④Teacher portrays the giant and reads those lines as well.

⑤Ask students to stand up and begin performing the story.

Note: If you have two teachers, one teacher can narrate the story and the other can play the giant.

Jumping Bean Story

Once upon a time there were a bunch of magical jumping beans, and they jumped and jumped and jumped and jumped and jumped.

Then, they fell over and said, "Ouch! I fell right on my bottom!"

They all stood up, and then they jumped and jumped and jumped and jumped and jumped, until they came to a huge beanstalk.

The jumping beans took a hold of the huge stalk, and they counted to ten as they climbed up to the top. "One, two, three, four, five, six, seven, eight, nine, ten!"

They jumped off the stalk and looked around.
"Look over there!" they said, "It's the giant's castle, let's go!"
So they jumped and jumped and jumped and jumped and jumped.

When they got to the door of the castle, they knocked three times, "Knock! Knock! Knock!"
"Who's there?" asked the giant.
"It's the magical jumping beans." they said.
The giant said, "Well come on in. I was just making some lunch."

So they jumped and jumped and jumped and sat down for lunch.
"Excuse me giant, WE'RE HUNGRY!" said the magical jumping beans as they held their bellies.

"How about some delicious macaroni and cheese?" asked the giant.
"Yummy!" said the jumping beans.

Then the giant gave everyone a big scoop of mac and cheese.
The jumping beans ate and ate and ate and ate until they all said, "Giant, we're thirsty."

"Would you like some fresh squeezed lemonade?" asked the giant.
"Yes please," said the jumping beans.

So the giant poured the lemonade.
And they drank and drank and drank and drank and drank it all up.

The jumping beans stretched up and let out a sigh, "Giant, we're tired," they said.

"Why don't you rest here for a while," said the giant.
"I'll wake you up after a short nap."
So the jumping beans lied down, fell asleep, and began to snore.

Suddenly, the giant's alarm clock went off, "RING! RING!"
The jumping beans woke up and said, "Giant, we're tired!"

"Okay, sleep a little longer," said the giant.
So the jumping beans fell asleep again and started to snore.

(Pause) "RING! RING!" Went the alarm again.
The jumping beans woke up and said, "Giant, we're tired!"
"Okay, okay, go back to sleep," said the giant.
Once again, the jumping beans went to sleep. (Pause)

This time when the alarm clock rang, "RING! RING!"
The jumping beans woke up and said, "Giant, we're awake!"

Then they jumped up and brushed their teeth, washed their face, combed their hair, looked at their watches and said, "Oh dear, look at the time! We're going to be late! Goodbye giant!"

The giant said, "Goodbye, my friends!" and waved as the jumping beans jumped out of the castle." The jumping beans said, "Thanks for lunch!"

The jumping beans jumped and jumped and jumped and jumped right back to the beanstalk.

They climbed down the beanstalk, counting backwards.
"Ten, nine, eight, seven, six, five, four, three, two, one!"
They jumped to the ground and said, "We did it!"

Then they jumped and jumped and jumped and jumped all the way home. And that is the story of the Magical Jumping Beans.

Everyone please take a bow!

Objective: Narrate a full-length story for the class to perform.

★ Jumping Bean Treasure

How to play

①Start with students sitting down for instructions.

②Tell students that they're going to perform the "Jumping Bean Treasure" story.

③Teacher reads the story and the students portray the jumping beans, repeating the lines.

④The teacher also plays the giant and reads those lines.

⑤Ask students to stand up and begin performing the story.

Jumping Bean Treasure Story

Once upon a time, there was a bunch of magical jumping beans, and they jumped and jumped and jumped and jumped and jumped.

Then, they fell over and said, "Ouch! I fell right on my bottom!"

They all stood up, and then they jumped and jumped and jumped and jumped and jumped. Until they came to a huge beanstalk, with a map attached to it.
"What could this be?" they said, "We should ask the giant!"

The jumping beans took the map and climbed the huge stalk.
As they climbed up, they counted to ten, "One, two, three, four, five, six, seven, eight, nine, ten!"

They jumped off the stalk and looked around.
"Look over there!" they said, "There's the Giant's castle, let's jump over to it."
So they jumped and jumped and jumped and jumped and jumped.

When they got to the door of the castle, they knocked three times, "Knock! Knock! Knock!"
"Who's there?" asked the giant.
"It's the magical jumping beans!" they said.

The giant said, "The jumping beans! It's fe fi foe fabulous to see you!"

"We need help!" said the jumping beans as they held up the map.
"What's this map?" asked the giant.
"We don't know." said the jumping beans.
The giant took the map and said, "This is a treasure map."
The jumping beans said, "A treasure map?"

"Would you like to search for the treasure?" asked the giant.
"Yes, right away!" said the jumping beans.

So they searched and searched and searched and searched and searched for hours.
The jumping beans stretched up and let out a sigh,
"Giant, it's been hours, we feel sleepy."

"Why don't you rest here for a while?" said the giant.
"I'll wake you up after a short nap and we'll find that treasure."
So the jumping beans fell asleep and began to snore.

The giant's alarm clock went off, "RING! RING!"
The jumping beans woke up and said, "Giant, we're tired!"

"Okay, you can sleep a little longer," said the giant.
So the jumping beans fell asleep again. (Pause) "RING! RING!"

The jumping beans woke up and said, "Giant, we're tired!"
"Okay, okay, go back to sleep, but not too long. We need to find the treasure!" The jumping beans went to sleep and began to snore. (Pause)
"RING! RING!"

This time when the alarm clock rang, the jumping beans got up quickly. They brushed their teeth, washed their face, and combed their hair.

Suddenly, as the jumping beans looked out in the distance, they noticed something and said, "Giant look over here!" The giant thundered over to the jumping beans and saw a big X.
"X marks the spot" said the giant. "Let's dig for it!" they all said.

So they dug and dug and dug and dug and dug, until they struck a treasure chest buried in the ground.

The giant said, "Let's lift it out together!"

They lifted up the heavy chest and opened it up. Inside there was enough treasure for all the jumping beans to share.

"This is the best!" said the jumping beans.
The sun was beginning to set. "We better get home, it's almost dark," said the jumping beans.

The giant said, "Goodbye my friends!" and waved from the castle.
The jumping beans said, "Thanks for the treasure!"

So the jumping beans jumped and jumped and jumped and jumped right back to the beanstalk.

They climbed down, counting backwards. "Ten, nine, eight, seven, six, five, four, three, two, one!" They jumped to the ground and said, "That was fun!"

Then they jumped and jumped and jumped and jumped all the way home with their treasure. And that is the story of the Jumping Bean Treasure.

Everyone please take a bow!

Objective: Narrate a full-length story for the class to perform.

Changing the world one child at a time

Play-Ground Theatre ®

Play-Ground Theatre

Part Two

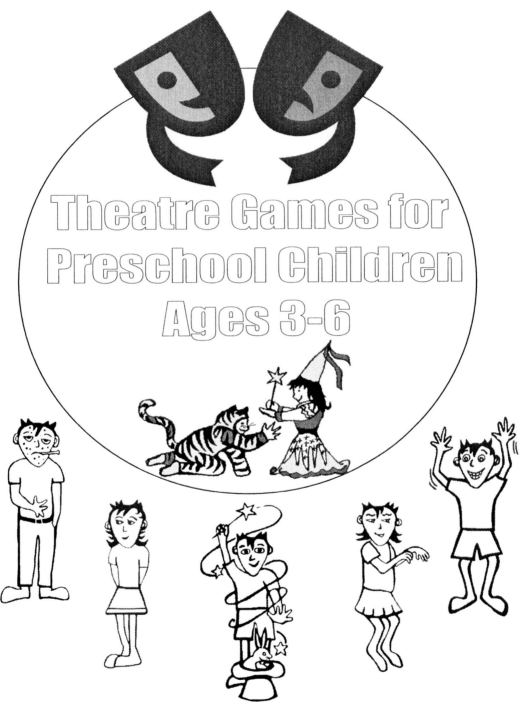

Color & Act - Emotions

Happy

Act  Happy

1. Flash a big, bright smile and laugh out loud to act happy.

2. Sing a song or whistle a tune to act happy.

3. Dance around the room to act happy.

4. Skip across the floor to act happy.

5. Cheer and clap your hands to act happy.

www.playgroundtheatre.com

Sad

Act  Sad

1. Curl down the corners of your mouth and frown to act sad.

2. Rub your eyes and let out a cry to act sad.

3. Hang your arms low to act sad.

4. Close your eyes and moan to act sad.

5. Sit down and pout to act sad.

www.playgroundtheatre.com

Surprised

Act Surprised

1. Open your eyes wide to act surprised.

2. Gasp to act surprised.

3. Jump up in the air to act surprised.

4. Put your hands over your mouth to act surprised.

5. Wake up from a dream and act surprised.

Angry

Act  Angry

1. Clench your fists to act angry.

2. Scrunch your face and growl to act angry.

3. Stomp your feet around the room to act angry.

4. Shake your head from side to side to act angry.

5. Put your hands on your waist to act angry.

www.playgroundtheatre.com

Cool

Act  Cool

1. Pretend to put on sunglasses and a backwards cap to act cool.

2. Walk down the street to act cool.

3. Wave to friends and say, "hello" to act cool.

4. Strut across the dance floor to act cool.

5. Talk to a friend on your cell phone to act cool.

www.playgroundtheatre.com

Excited

Act  Excited

1. Smile and giggle to act excited.

2. Lift up your hands and wave them in the air to act excited.

3. Wiggle your body to act excited.

4. Give someone a big smile and share your joy to act excited

5. Jump up and down to act excited.

www.playgroundtheatre.com

Silly

Act  Silly

1. Make five funny faces to act silly.

2. Hop on one foot to act silly.

3. Dance around and make hilarious sounds to act silly.

4. Bump into things to act silly.

5. Slip and fall down on the ground to act silly.

www.playgroundtheatre.com

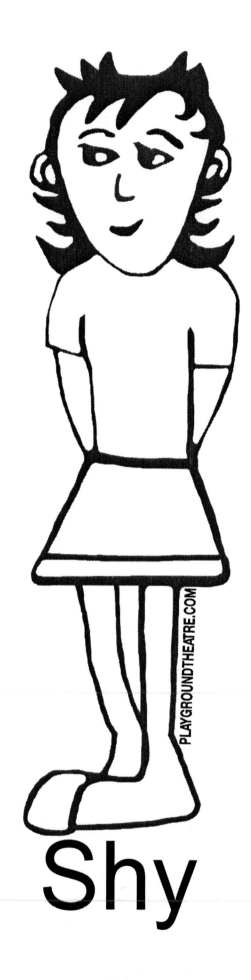

Shy

Act  Shy

1. Hide your face with your hands to act shy.

2. Sit quietly and close your eyes to act shy.

3. Whisper in a soft voice to act shy.

4. Hide behind a friend to act shy.

5. Say, "hello" in a soft voice to act shy.

www.playgroundtheatre.com

Afraid

Act  Afraid

1. Cover your eyes to act afraid.

2. Run away from a monster to act afraid.

3. Hide behind a chair to act afraid.

4. Let out a scream to act afraid.

5. Make your whole body quiver to act afraid.

www.playgroundtheatre.com

Sneaky

Act  Sneaky

1. Snicker out loud to act sneaky.

2. Walk without making a sound to act sneaky.

3. Quickly hide to act sneaky.

4. Tip toe around to act sneaky.

5. Duck down low and crawl to act sneaky.

www.playgroundtheatre.com

Stubborn

Act Stubborn

1. Fold your arms to act stubborn.

2. Shake your head to act stubborn.

3. Stomp your foot down to act stubborn.

4. Say "NO" to act stubborn.

5. Sit down and grunt to act stubborn.

www.playgroundtheatre.com

Sick

Act  Sick

1. Make your head heavy and take your temperature to act sick.

2. Cover your mouth and cough to act sick.

3. Sneeze three times to act sick.

4. Rub your belly to act sick.

5. Lie down and rest to act sick.

www.playgroundtheatre.com

Magical

Act Magical

1. Wiggle your fingers to act magical.

2. Fly around the room to act magical.

3. Perform a trick to act magical.

4. Make a secret wish to act magical.

5. Disappear into thin air to act magical.

www.playgroundtheatre.com

Cold

Act  Cold

1. Chatter your teeth to act cold.

2. Wrap up in a blanket to act cold.

3. Shake in your boots to act cold.

4. Pretend to put on your winter coat and gloves to act cold.

5. Rub your hands together and blow on them to act cold.

www.playgroundtheatre.com

Hot

Act  Hot

1. Wipe sweat off your forehead to act hot.

2. Crawl through the desert to act hot.

3. Breathe in and out quickly to act hot.

4. Swallow water and quench your thirst to act hot.

5. Walk quickly over sand to act hot.

www.playgroundtheatre.com

Bonus Materials
Learning with Animals

Animal Matching Game
Animal Spelling Game
Animal Counting Game

Make copies of the following exercises.

Animal Matching Game

Draw a line from the animal name to the picture.

Dog

Fish

Tiger

Dolphin

Duck

Lizard

www.playgroundtheatre.com

Animal Matching Game

Draw a line from the animal name to the picture.

Butterfly

Alligator

Bat

Kangaroo

Camel

Chicken

Spider

www.playgroundtheatre.com

Animal Matching Game

Draw a line from the name to the animal picture.

Unicorn

Lion

Crab

Bear

Pig

Mouse

www.playgroundtheatre.com

Animal Matching Game

Draw a line from the name to the animal picture.

Bumble Bee

Frog

Snake

Dinosaur

Rabbit

Turtle

www.playgroundtheatre.com

Animal Spelling Game

Spell the animal name in the blank spaces provided.

____ ____ ____

____ ____ ____

____ ____ ____

____ ____ ____ ____

____ ____ ____ ____

____ ____ ____ ____

Animal Spelling Game

Spell the animal name in the blank spaces provided.

Animal Spelling Game

Spell the animal name in the blank spaces provided.

__ __ __ __ __

__ __ __ __ __ __

__ __ __ __ __ __

__ __ __ __ __ __ __

__ __ __ __ __ __

__ __ __ __ __ __ __ __

www.playgroundtheatre.com

Animal Spelling Game

Spell the animal name in the blank spaces provided.

_ _ _ _ _ _ _ _ _ _ _

_ _ _ _ _ _ _ _ _ _

_ _ _ _ _ _ _ _ _ _ _

_ _ _ _ _ _ _ _ _ _

_ _ _ _ _ _ _ _ _ _ _

_ _ _ _ _ _ _ _ _ _

_ _ _ _ _ _ _ _ _ _ _

www.playgroundtheatre.com

Animal Counting Game

Count the number of animals below and fill in the blank.

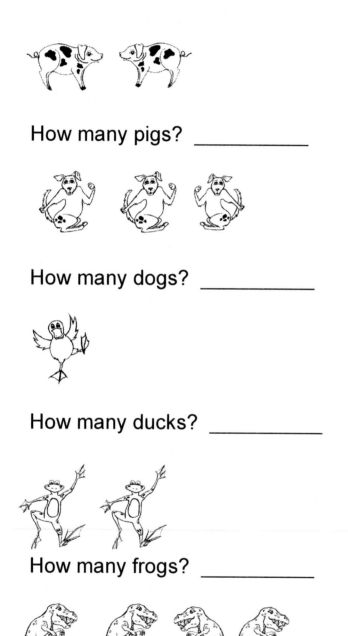

How many pigs? _____

How many dogs? _____

How many ducks? _____

How many frogs? _____

How many dinosaurs? _____

www.playgroundtheatre.com

Animal Counting Game

Count the number of animals below and fill in the blank.

How many turtles? _____

How many bats? _____

How many bumble bees? _____

How many bears? _____

How many rabbits? _____

www.playgroundtheatre.com

Animal Counting Game

Count the number of animals below and fill in the blank.

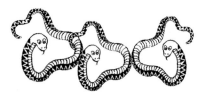

How many snakes? _____

How many chickens? _____

How many alligators? _____

How many kangaroos? _____

How many butterflies? _____

Animal Counting Game

Count the number of animals below and fill in the blank.

How many lizards? _____

How many lions? _____

How many fish? _____

How many unicorns? _____

How many dolphins? _____

www.playgroundtheatre.com

Animal Counting Game

Count the number of animals below and fill in the blank.

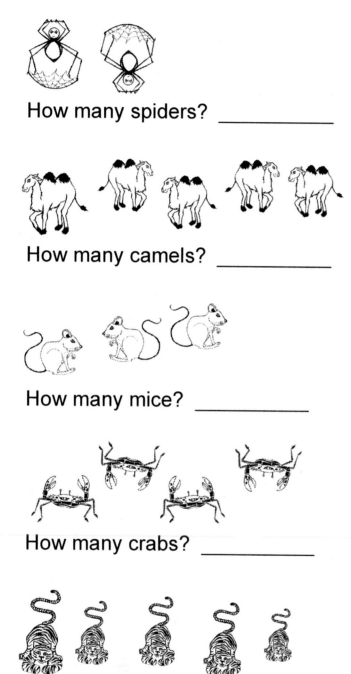

How many spiders? _____

How many camels? _____

How many mice? _____

How many crabs? _____

How many tigers? _____

www.playgroundtheatre.com

Answer Key

Animal Matching Game
Animal Spelling Game
Animal Counting Game

www.playgroundtheatre.com

Animal Matching Game

Answer Key

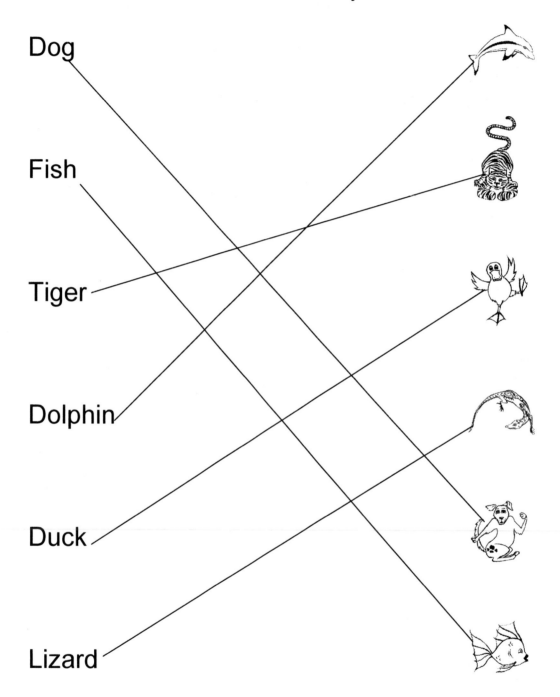

Dog

Fish

Tiger

Dolphin

Duck

Lizard

Animal Matching Game

Answer Key

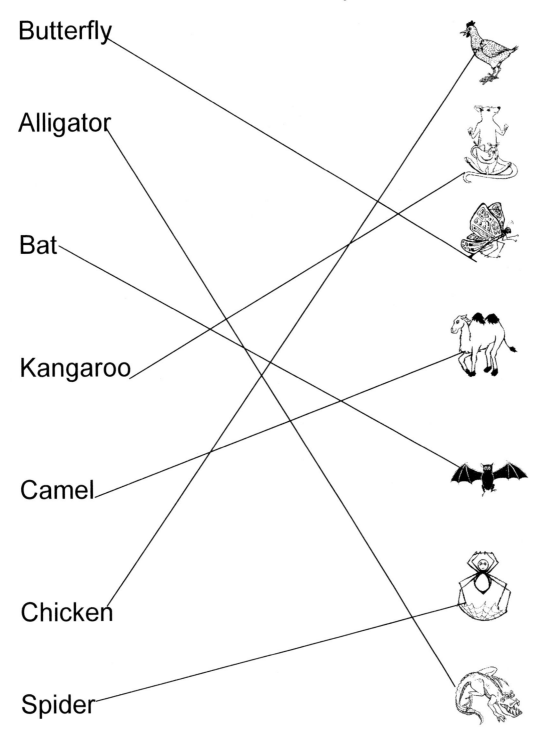

Butterfly

Alligator

Bat

Kangaroo

Camel

Chicken

Spider

www.playgroundtheatre.com

Animal Matching Game

Answer Key

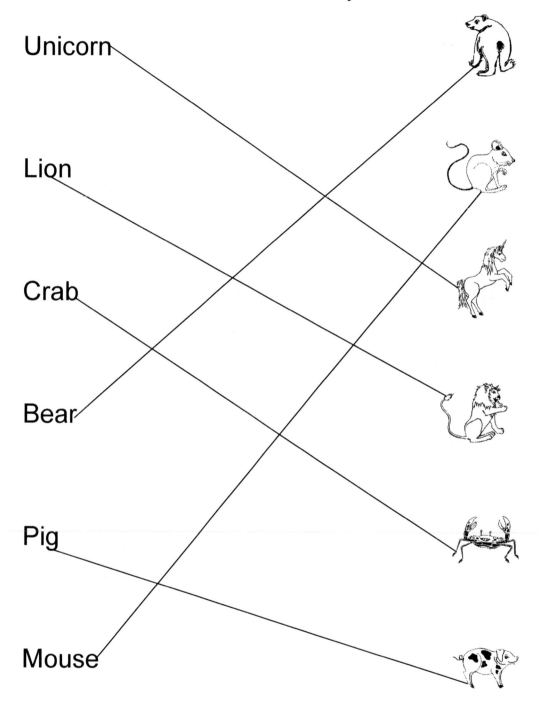

Unicorn

Lion

Crab

Bear

Pig

Mouse

www.playgroundtheatre.com

Animal Matching Game

Answer Key

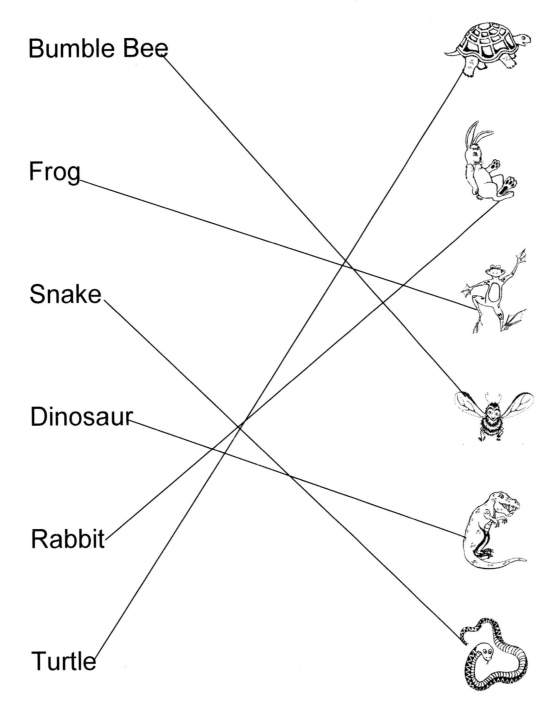

Bumble Bee

Frog

Snake

Dinosaur

Rabbit

Turtle

www.playgroundtheatre.com

Animal Spelling Game

Answer Key

 D O G

 P I G

 B A T

 F R O G

 B E A R

 D U C K

www.playgroundtheatre.com

Animal Spelling Game

Answer Key

 C R A B

 L I O N

 F I S H

 T I G E R

 C A M E L

 S N A K E

www.playgroundtheatre.com

Animal Spelling Game

Answer Key

 M O U S E

 L I Z A R D

 S P I D E R

 **T U R T L E**

 R A B B I T

 D O L P H I N

www.playgroundtheatre.com

Animal Spelling Game

Answer Key

 C H I C K E N

 U N I C O R N

K A N G A R O O

 D I N O S A U R

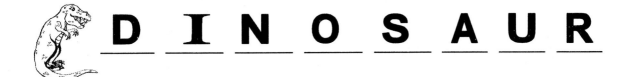 B U T T E R F L Y

 A L L I G A T O R

 B U M B L E B E E

www.playgroundtheatre.com

Animal Counting Game

Answer Key

How many pigs? **2**

How many dogs? **3**

How many ducks? **1**

How many frogs? **2**

How many dinosaurs? **4**

www.playgroundtheatre.com

- 144 -

Animal Counting Game

Answer Key

How many turtles? _____ **3**_____

How many bats? _____ **5**_____

How many bumble bees? _**2**_____

How many bears? _____ **3**_____

How many rabbits? _____ **4**_____

www.playgroundtheatre.com

Animal Counting Game

Answer Key

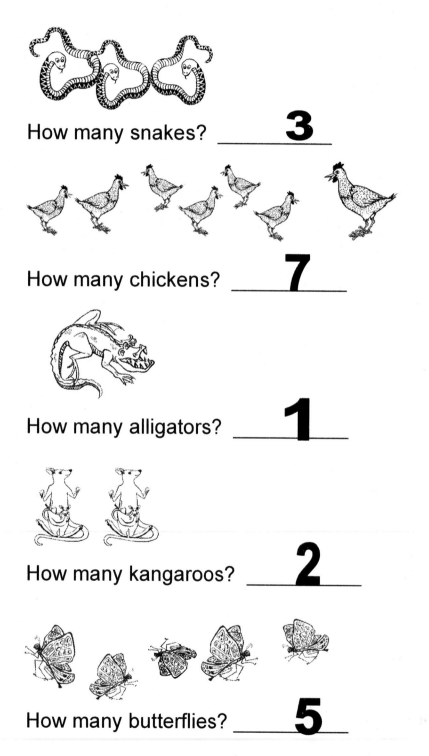

How many snakes? _____ **3**_____

How many chickens? _____ **7**_____

How many alligators? _____ **1**_____

How many kangaroos? _____ **2**_____

How many butterflies? _____ **5**_____

www.playgroundtheatre.com

Animal Counting Game

Answer Key

How many lizards? **4**

How many lions? **3**

How many fish? **6**

How many unicorns? **5**

How many dolphins? **4**

www.playgroundtheatre.com

Animal Counting Game

Answer Key

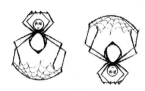

How many spiders? _____**2**_____

How many camels? _____**5**_____

How many mice? _____**3**_____

How many crabs? _____**4**_____

How many tigers? _____**5**_____

www.playgroundtheatre.com

Special Thanks to illustrators & contributors:
Katrina van Pelt, Todd Bryan, Andy Seery, Anupam Rai,
Julie Ikler, and Louise Fordyce.

Meet the Authors and Founders of Play-Ground Theatre Company, Inc. Mia Sole & Jeff Haycock

Madcap. Energetic. Joyful. These are just a few of the adjectives that come instantly to mind when describing Mia Sole and Jeff Haycock, founders of Colorado's Play-Ground Theatre Company. They began writing, directing, and performing plays in the spirit of "Saturday Night Live" for kids, while providing acting workshops for all ages in 1989.

Over the years, Play-Ground Theatre's performances, and programs for children have become increasingly popular. As they considered ways of meeting children's needs, they realized that they had been developing a curriculum to share – a program that captures the spirit of Play-Ground Theatre.

They now offer educators a drama program for preschool children ages 3-6, and a school age drama program for ages 7-12. These theatre programs include: self-study training manuals, marketing kit, CDs of songs and music, text books with complete lesson plans, scripts, costume accessories, handouts, and summer drama books.

Play-Ground Theatre fosters not only a delight in the performing arts, but a powerful self-esteem which carries over into other activities and endeavors. Their motto is "Play-Ground Theatre: Changing the world one child at a time." Considering their successful work and play with children and adults, perhaps that motto should be revised to read: one *inner* child at a time.

For more information visit: www.playgroundtheatre.com
or call the Colorado Main Office at 303.258.0393

Play-Ground Theatre Preschool Drama Program for Ages 3-6

You can host an innovative, energizing, motivating, and financially successful drama program that teachers, students, and parents love. Play-Ground Preschool Drama Program for Ages 3-6 includes **everything** teachers need to easily make theatre a regular part of their classroom.

Training Manuals, Textbooks, Scripts, Costumes, Props, Music, Handouts, Summer Books and more! This program can be instructed during the school day or as an additional program after school.

Incorporate acting, dance, music, singing, performance, teamwork, and self-expression in a safe, positive environment. Students choose their own characters and perform plays with teachers for families and friends to enjoy. Preschool Drama Program for ages 3-6 is also available.

Contact: www.playgroundtheatre.com

Play-Ground Theatre Company, Inc.
Products & Services

Preschool Drama Program
For Ages 3-6
Complete Curriculum
$495
Staff Trainings Available
Call: 303.258.0393
More Information:
www.playgroundtheatre.com

School Age Drama Program
For Ages 7-12
Complete Curriculum
$495
Staff Trainings Available
Call: 303.258.0393
More Information:
www.playgroundtheatre.com

The Best of Play-Ground
Theatre on DVD

- 3 Billy Goats Gruff
- Sleeping Beauty
- Rappin' Red Riding Hood
- Return of the Dodo Bird
- Pirates Treasure
- The Space Crusaders

Available on-line now! $14.99
www.playgroundtheatre.com

THEATRE GAMES
FOR ELEMENTARY SCHOOL
CHILDREN AGES 7-12

FIRST EDITION

By Mia Sole & Jeff Haycock

$24.95 each
Bulk discounts available.
To order: www.playgroundtheatre.com

Wishing you great success with Play-Ground Theatre Company's

Theatre Games for Preschool Children Ages 3-6